Spinning the Arrow of Time

"Spinning the Arrow of Time *is powerfully impressive. As a theoretical physicist and poet I felt that it conveyed me to my innermost realm. Every poem touched not only my soul but also my intellect. Ruth understands the interconnectedness of everything in the physical world. She uses wondrous images, and her poems are deeply meaningful, open to multiple layers of interpretation. This book will be treasured by people who appreciate rich, nontraditional writing."*

—Steven Duplij, Fulbright Visiting Professor of Theoretical Physics, Rutgers University

"What a magnificent collection! Ruth Hoppin's poems inspire appreciation for celestial wonders, ancient spirits, dreams, tolerance, and resolute prayers as we weep for and rejoice in the place we call Earth."

—Teresa LeYung-Ryan, author of *Love Made of Heart*

"These evocative poems of past, present and future provide in-depth insight that is so needed in today's way of life."

—Albert M. Teglia, Mayor of Daly City, Retired

*"*Spinning the Arrow of Time *starts out great and gets better! It stirs the imagination and feeds the soul. It's a night gallery of thought-provoking verse for dreamers who still wish upon stars and see things not as they are but as how they could be. The myriad images are tightly woven into a patchwork quilt of faith and fanciful delight. Like a grandmaster, she has painted images that lesser poets will wish they had written. Her religious poems are especially well crafted and inspiring."*

—Clay Harrison, Virginia poet / lyricist

"Exploring our relationship to the universe, science, God, and one another, Spinning the Arrow of Time *captures the timeless connection between Creation, our faith, and our history. We are all interconnected, and I invite everyone to explore this through Ruth Hoppin's poems."*

—Rev. Jon Owens, Episcopal Diocese of California

"Ruth Hoppin uses language both spare and elegant to express her profound ideas. Along the way, her whimsical sense of humor will surely make you smile."

—Sue Bessmer, PhD, author, *How the World Worked: From the Pharaohs to Christopher Columbus*

Other Books by Ruth Hoppin

Priscilla's Letter

La Carta de Priscila
(Translated by Rev. Paul Benjamin Alfaro)

Spinning the Arrow of Time

Poems by Ruth Hoppin

LOST
COAST
PRESS

Spinning the Arrow of Time

Poems by Ruth Hoppin

Lost Coast Press
155 Cypress Street
Fort Bragg, CA 95437
(800) 773-7782
www.cypresshouse.com

Cover and Book design by Mike Brechner / Cypress House
Cover illustration: *The Myth of Time* © rolffimages – Fotolia.com

ISBN 978-1-935448-19-8
LCCN: 2012936533

Printed in the USA
2 4 6 8 9 7 5 3 1

To June and Ralph,

denizens of the space age

Acknowledgments

Some of the poems in this collection appeared previously as follows:

"Into Silence" and "Holy Spirit Interceding" (*Priscilla Papers)*

"A Writer's Prayer," "Poet's Quest," and "Emboldenment" (*The Christian Communicator)*

A shorter version of "The Magi Quest" (reprinted from *Lifting Women's Voices: Prayers to Change the World* by permission of Church Publishing, Incorporated, Harrisburg, PA, 2009.

"Retreat" (*The National Christian Reporter)*

"Vision Quest" (*Christian Meditation Newsletter, The World Community for Christian Meditation US Update)*

"Contemplation" (*Contemplative Prayer Outreach News)*

"Leaving Ireland" (*The Review of Language and Culture)*

"Under the Sea" (*Fandangle Magazine)*

"Colored Balloons" (*The Land of Nod)*

Contents

Spinning the Arrow of Time

Though nations may vanish
in mists of time,
dare spin the arrow
it is no crime;
the future is far
the future is near
spin the arrow
and have no fear.

Now the arrow of time is spun;
what have we done?
Women and men who lived before
will they live again?
Boys and girls who have not been born
will they rule the world?
Come wait with me with bated breath
to see where the arrow will come to rest.

I

Escaping the Bonds of Earth

A Land of True Belonging

Stars and planets are to me a sign
they light my way to worlds divine
though earth betoken the home of longing
I look to a land of true belonging.

Borne on a sweet resounding chord
a song from beyond enthralls me
I dream of a world that is unexplored,
a faraway land that calls me.

Siren Song of Infinity

What is the siren song of infinity —
its lure
that claims us for its own
and still seeks more?

First its distant tones
turn our cares away
from our ancestral home,
cause our thoughts to stray

far beyond the mountains
far beyond the sky
where mind cannot imagine,
stars themselves may die;

then it gives us daring
to follow where it calls
where distance is unsparing,
universes fall —

past earth, till earth is gone
with faint, unsmiling face;
do you hear the siren song?
do you long to follow us?

Space Travel

Far from the old familiar ground
let the earth be turned around
underneath a higher dome
a wider sky than home
Let distance tell us what is true
while silence and space keep rendezvous
over the vastness— guardian twins—
a world ends and one begins
time fades, scattered stillness reigns.

Like angels borne on cosmic wings
bent with universal sight
to probe the outer rim of night
or spirits from the body fled
to climb the heights of heaven instead,
joyous in the sky we hover
not one, but many worlds discover
and see the old familiar ground
with unaccustomed grandeur crowned.

Delegate

The spacecraft Voyager I, on a mission to Jupiter
and beyond, is likely destined to drift endlessly in space.

Envoy of the human race
whose quest for knowledge sets your pace
in our stead we bid you go:
You shall traverse a holy field
that mysteries may be revealed,
brave sentinel of space.

Far-flung shadow of the mind
and collective will of humankind:
You are steady, keen and sure
in places we cannot endure
where knowledge lies in distant skies
with burning orbits intertwined.

Go, seek the last frontier of learning
the farthest point of no returning:
Somewhere on the cosmic sea
by lonely starlight shall it be
that our search for truth is ended
with your life for truth expended.

On the Extinction of Matter Near a Black Hole

Atomic particles
dance like clowns
on the brink of shaking
the ultimate bond;
into the vortex catapulting
over the edge with strange exulting.
These are spawned a paradigm
of all the progeny of time
whose fate is sealed
in the drift of stars,
strewn like the roll of a trillion dice,
lighted like candles on a cake
to be extinguished one by one
to vanish, perchance, or to be reborn.

In a Darkling Hour

A dream is born in a darkling hour
in a deep spell, in mystical power
by incantation, swiftly glides
supernal over moonstruck tides.

Bid the mythic moment stay
to conjure the past — hold sway
with dream-vision; let it survey
bold pageants of yesterday.

In a darkling hour when mind retires
a dreamer lights mystic fires
along a steep and high patrol
to ransom his imprisoned soul.

What incredible magic is here —
through time and space a thoroughfare!
A quaint tableau is about to begin
the future comes trooping in

with cheerful mien, bravely unrolls
victories burnished on hidden scrolls —
astounding mysteries of grace —
while dreamfire glows on his raptured face.

At length the dazzling momentum is stayed
radiance pales, images fade
the present asserts pragmatic claim
shatters the spell, damps the flame.

The sparkling hour will soon be gone
when past and future seem as one;
Before it subsides, the charm recanted,
high on the moontide another is chanted.

II

Space Age Diplomacy

Repartee

Earthling: Your eyes are orange
your skin is blue
I've never seen
the likes of you.
Alien: Your eyes are brown
your skin is white
you have two ears!
you look a sight.
Earthling: You nab us, jab us
treat us rough
go home, we don't
like that stuff.
Alien: Why do you want
to start a fight?
We can travel
faster than light.
Earthling: *We* know how
to level a curse
Stay in your part
of the universe!

Quandary

I don't know if their skin is green
these strange ones I have never seen
if I meet them on my way
should I go with them or stay?

They have come from such a distance
should I go at their insistence?
are they charming — in their way?
should I go or should I stay?

If I stay because of doubt
maybe I'll be missing out
if I go with green-skinned men
I'll never see my friends again.

Star People

Star people, do you live forever?
travel to and fro in time?
stop your spaceship on a dime?
tour infinity? Oh, how clever!

Star people, do you have a mission
to defend us from our folly;
to befriend us and be jolly
then to give an admonition?

Far Out

In the future for diversion
let us take a space excursion —
what adventure shall be ours!
What bug-eyed bugs will give us hugs
as we travel to the stars!
Alien creatures from the deep
are bound to give a steady beep;
what fun to answer them in code —
then, to visit their abode
(only if they double dare us
and *if* they promise not to scare us)
think of all our new-found friends
by the time our journey ends!

When other forms of life assemble
who can say what they'll resemble?
I think I'll take some home with me
(if I can get them to agree) —
strangelings for the world to ponder
live mementos from out yonder;
at last with papers all in order
we shall cross the starry border
with happy memories of our trip
— foreign creatures in our grip —
listen for the farewell "blip"!

Star Colony

In space the factories are humming
this is where they'll soon be coming
migrants from the seven seas
streaming in like refugees
just because they were told that
Earth was getting slightly old-hat.

They must grow used to our ways
working fifty-hour days
space-time cards, unfamiliar labors —
and learn to like their weirdo neighbors.
I can see bridges burning,
a long commute with no returning.

Homesick

I wanted to get away from it all
well, I did
land on the moon was up for sale
I put in my bid.
Now I wish I had only rented.
I don't know why I was discontented
or why I live on a satellite
when the big old earth is shining bright.

If I were to go on a distant trek
where earth was only a tiny speck
a million million miles away
would I find a happier place to stay —
in a different part of the galaxy —
or learn how much earth meant to me?

III

A Mind of Their Own

The Sun — A Sol-iloquy

I never set on my domain
(all to lose, nothing to gain)
I shudder to think of the instant crash
all my colonies gone in a flash,

who in turn must never secede
(they must listen, they must heed)
it is written in the sky:
"The day you rebel is the day you die."

I don't believe they want to be free
Earth still harbors affection for me
giving me credit for sunny days
though no more processions, songs and praise.

I miss the old days and the hoopla
when I was the great sun god Ra
I miss the old ways, the solar chic
the pageantry, the bold mystique;

Times have changed, what remains?
My beneficial rule sustains
keeps them in their proper place
with solar *flair* they can't efface.

Earth Responds

It must seem to the blazing sun
it doesn't pay to be the one
to stoke the furnace and make the weather
trying to keep it all together;
splitting atoms — an endless chore
producing sunlight — mainly a bore —
the sun at the center continues to fry
while planets roll in a nice cool sky.

Planet for Sale

Mercury

Do you see that small planet
with the "FOR SALE" sign on it?
So far there is no buyer
the climate is dire
by day it is 660 degrees
at night you freeze
at minus 200 — that's cold
maybe that's why it hasn't been sold.
Its next-door neighbor
is a holy terror
keeps trying to burn the house down
though arson is hard to prove —
pray the planet is sold soon
the tenant is anxious to move.

Treadmill to Oblivion

Mercury

I seem to be going in circles
around the sun.
Track is my favorite sport
I clock in at one hundred ten thousand miles per hour
by last report;
No matter how fast I run
I seem to be going in circles
around the sun.

P.S.
It's so boring here
each day is like 2/3 of a year.

Heartthrob

Venus

I won a beauty contest
when first the world was finished
five billion years ago —
my charm is undiminished;
Upon my brow I wear thick clouds
which give me much protection
against the heat that otherwise
would ruin my complexion;
They guarantee the same allure
that won the heart of the dinosaur
will keep me looking like a star
to all who see me from afar.

The Favored One

Venus

In mythology, Mercury was the Messenger of the Gods,
Venus the Goddess of Love, and Mars the God of War.

Of all the planets near the sun
I must be the favored one.

Mercury races to sound the alarm
I have all there is of charm.

Earth seeks me out till I am found
Says I make the world go round.

Mars is warlike, aids the fighter
I fill the heart to make it lighter.

Reflections on a Martian Landscape

This is where empires crumble
before they are ever begun —
on a planet that wandered
beyond the warmth of the sun —
this is where dreams are undone.

Upon the barren land
rocks are scattered round
as if some daring plan
lay shattered on the ground —
a monument to kings
who never will be crowned.

This is where futile hopes
are mingled with the dust,
rise to meet alien skies
like mournful ghosts.

The Flood

What was the surface like before
the day the ice began to thaw
freed for a time by the sun's decree
or shaken by some catastrophe
to storm and batter the whole terrain —
what perished there on the flooded plain?

Could there be life on planet Mars
simpler and more tenacious than ours—
A soul that once was terrified
thought the storm would not subside
yet clung to life and held its ground
in the wild tempest that hurled it around?

Do we detect a haunting trace
of waters that lashed the planet's face?
Deep etched lines like constant frowning
in arid rock, a fear of drowning
in the primal mind of a life form, mingling
with echoes of primeval singing?

Reflections of the Moon — First Moonwalk

With face averted, I sought to hide
that which lurked in my darker side
a shadow bordering on despair
captive to a happier sphere,

Reflecting light not my own —
how could it reach and make whole
deep recesses of my soul
all the darker — and alone?

Then to my dim, stark territory
there came a day of laughter and glory —
of banners waved and words engraved
while a great companion planet raved.

The clamorous joy of their arrival
was something akin to religious revival
my spirit arose from a barren land
to hold the soul of a world in my hand.

I go on my way forever bearing
imprint of high desire and daring
reflecting light not from the sun —
Spirit-light from a brave deed done.

Reflections of the Moon —
Keeper of the Night

I am more than a satellite
I am a lantern in the night
over a world where eyes are bright
turning upward at the sight.

I love to pose with changing mien
I love to make them smile
slow pirhouetting to be seen
I know they love my style.

With gentle glow upon my brow
I will ever turn and glide
I tug at the heart of a world —
and turn the tide.

Jupiter

Jupiter is jolly and fat
tries to diet but balloons up
and that's that —
always was the biggest planet
I doubt if roads will ever span it
yet it wears a pleasant grin
inviting spacemen to come in
check the furniture for dust
hunt for microbes if they must —
though stout the planet is beguiling
a bit far out, but keeps on smiling.

Jupiter's Moons

"Mother" Earth has *one* moon
that's terrific!
I've sixty plus —
who's more prolific?
I am proud I gave them birth
they are known as far as Earth.

Europa is a celebrity
Io —
Callisto — let them be
none totally
eclipses me.

I often tell them
fame is spurious
folk on Earth
are cold and curious:
who gave us names
like "Ganymede"?
how can we be Greek?
Indeed!
They go their way
I let them roam
They can't escape
The pull of home.

Titan Speaks

Data from Voyager I's journey to Saturn and its moons reveals the diameter of Titan to be 5140 kilometers, placing it second to Jupiter's moon Ganymede by a narrow margin. Titan's atmosphere, like that of Earth, consists largely of nitrogen.

I say fie, a thousand times fie
for watching me with beady eye,
talking about my atmosphere
as if you think I cannot hear.

You call my ambience dark and dreary
that's an unconstructive theory
I have nitrogen — more than Earth
you must know what that is worth;
often through the mist and haze
a view of Saturn cheers my days.

You say that life is frozen out
do you know that beyond doubt?
We have microbes, lowly now
they're evolving and know how
beneath my polar clouds of ice
where the weather will suffice.

Now check your data — it's misleading
as concerns my relative size
(or some earthling is misreading) —
I am the largest moon in the skies —
a status I am not conceding
just because your figures lie
I say fie, a thousand times fie
on spacecraft sent to snoop and spy!

Saturn

Saturn is much maligned
by the epithet "saturnine"
applied to folk
on all sorts of downers
who never joke,
and constant frowners.

Saturn is full of cheer
Saturn likes to float in air,
spin on its axis
faster and faster
around the sun —
this is fun!
Saturn has rings 'n things
Saturn swings.

Non-Conformity

Hyperion, an odd-shaped moon of Saturn, has been described variously as a "potato," a "fossil tooth," or a "dented beer can" in appearance.

My shape is odd
I don't fit in
with any of the rules
you've written.
If you ask why
I'd say "because";
I'll live and die
by my own laws.

Let other moons
be smooth and fawn
for me the day
will never dawn
that I'm into
conformity
the way I am
is the way I'll be
not what you
expect of me.

The Disappearance

Jupiter and Saturn disappeared from the night sky in September, 1981. They were on the other side of the sun and were not seen again until 2000.

Saturn and Jupiter, where have you gone?
We have gone to the other side of the sun.

When will mortals feast their eyes on
two who slipped past our horizon?

In the year 2000 as you reckon
we'll see the homeward cycle beckon.

I bid you Godspeed in your journeys
and hope to greet the two returnees.

Uranus

In Greek mythology, Uranus is the personification of heaven.

Heaven is just a name
this place is much the same
as other worlds begun
that drift with clouds
follow the crowds
play hide-and-seek with the sun;
Dazed when meteors veer
amazed when comets flare
I wonder how it feels
to breathe in finer air
and spin my wheels
to mark another year.

Neptune

God Of The Sea

Sparkling lakes
foamy brine
are the fixtures of my shrine
at my altar by the sea
where laughing children
splash with glee.
Deepest waters
of the ocean
are the measure of devotion
to a bounding deity
whom the people all adore;
On the tossing crest of waves
that dare the storm
there Neptune saves,
brings them safely to the shore.
I will say until I die
"Neptune's planet sails the sky."

Transformation

One physicist theorizes that extremely high temperatures and pressure on Neptune may have converted carbon to diamonds. The result could be small diamond flakes drifting through the atmosphere or forming a surface layer.

By miracle of high compression
lowly carbon from the sod
finds new and lovelier expression
in Neptune's glittering façade.

Not by mining or invention
not by labor , slave or free;
patterned by a high intention,
sown with liberality.

Strewn like winter's cache of snowflakes
falling in a prodigal scheme —
confetti sequins on a landscape
whose lavish beauty reigns supreme —
diamonds drift and deepen like snow
to make the jeweled planet glow.

God shakes the snowflakes from the sky
cascading on the mountainside
carved in ice, plied with lace
glistening as they coalesce,
presses carbon from the ground
by a similar impulse bound
until its nature is realigned;

Because it sparkles with new-found grace
the face of nature is redesigned.

Pluto

Pluto, known also as Hades, is the planet that symbolizes death. The outermost planet in our solar system, its orbit swung inside that of Neptune on January 22, 1979 for the first time in 248 years. Their positions reversed in March, 1999.

This is the outermost bound; come see
that to which all is progressing
in fiery blast; in orbital path
of planets retrogressing.

This is the end of the line; proceed
beyond this boundary, who dares
to know the outcome of his deeds
and face the spectre of his fears.

The Comet as Seen from Earth

Delinquent star
careening around the sun
as if to blaze
a trail to oblivion:
we fear your lawless ways —
your forays into space —
We know a planet's track
a moon that stays sedately back:
so when you run your private race
then disappear without a trace
here we view you with surmise
speculate on your demise
until, unchastened by the years,
a flaming herald reappears,
sweeps its torch across our skies.

The Comet as Seen from Heaven

You hail the stars
who blink in reply
with icy eyes
as you pass them by.
In empty space
with no sure guide
except your daring
you light up the sky.
You set up a flare
to mark your flight
swiftly glide
with steady sight
and celestial glow
that redeems the night.

The Quark

The quark is a subatomic particle with a characteristic described as "charm."

I brighten the world
of subatomic particles
constantly bombarded by protons
sent shrieking into oblivion
or escaping into the crevices of time;
shot down in a random course
or self-destructing without a thought;
Even here
on the cruel frontier of science
there is a place for that subtle influence
I exert:
I flirt.

Judgment

The universe seems to be expanding at an ever-increasing speed as galaxies move further apart.

Behold the speeding constellations
fleeing the wrath of warring nations
they cannot abide
Earth's wickedness and fratricide;
they would travel faster if they could
to get away from the neighborhood.

IV

Earth's Past

How Life Originated

According to an influential theory, methane, ammonia and water molecules in the sea — a primordial broth — were energized by ultraviolet radiation to form amino acids, the building blocks of proteins.

When sky encircled a murky view
over a sea of molecular stew
one of the canny molecules rose
and said to the others: "On your toes!"

"Today we have no identity
tomorrow we'll be an entity;
alone we are stuck in primordial soup
together we'll be a regular group!"

Front and center, with great elan
dance of the molecules began
with an allemande left and a dos-a-do
soon they were standing in a row.

Whether by accident or design
another and another joined the line
with an allemande right and a dos-a-dos
they shimmied away the status quo.

Now they are complex molecules
chanting in unison "Protein *rules!*"

History as It Might Have Been

According to one theory, men from outer space mated with Neanderthal women, producing the superior Cro-Magnon people and speeding up the process of evolution.

Behold on earth a motley crew
this is what we had to do:
it behooved to romance them
to improve them and advance them.

By ye gods, we never dreamt
to find such creatures, so unkempt
to mate with them was not a task
that we relished or would ask.

In spite of having high-brow daddies
many of the boys were baddies
hunted down and killed their brothers
primitive — just like their mothers.

This is not what we desired
only what history required.

Dar-win Loses

The Darwinian theory that new species of life arise gradually from their ancestors is coming under fire. New evidence indicates that species appear suddenly in geological time and change little for millions of years.

In ages past we were holy
no one thought we evolved slowly
now the world in mighty chorus
proclaims a lower species bore us.

Bits of bone and rock-bound fossil
evidence appears colossal
yet not everyone agrees
that our forebears swung from trees

With massive jaw and tiny brain
or vestiges that still remain
simian brow and mouth agape
all the features of an ape;

some say the ape is not our cousin
and Darwin's theory is unproven!
In our heart of hearts we knew
oh yes, we knew it all along

this was not the way to go
Darwin didn't have a song:
We were made by a higher power
finished, I think, in less than an hour.

An Archaeologist's Dream

While the days go round and round
memories stir beneath the ground
ancient spirits wonder when
their glory will be known again.

Where their children's feet once stumbled
over rocks now white and crumbled
they return with eyes unseeing
by the magnet of the mind
to the structure of their being
by the timeless rocks defined;
memory clings to the granite mound
while the years go round and round.

The spirits wait for a tapping sound
a light in the eyes of eager souls
who will sift the hallowed dust of their homes
enshrined in the earth with their useless bones
deftly trace the former ways
thrill to the glory of olden days;
the spirits wait — for only then
shall the dead past rise to life again.

Ode to Atlantis

Some nations live beyond their prime
to keep a careful check on time
they see their ancient deeds applauded
in solemn histories recorded;
Atlantis, buried in the sea,
lives only in our memory.

Its people in their silent plight
gather under evening skies
ghostly specters in the night
in mist and shadow they arise
while every moment newborn waves
dance and frolic on their graves.

What great cities did they build
with feats of architecture filled?
What vanished language served to bear
the mighty impulse of their prayer?

No marker points to their returning
or keeps a record of their learning;
in trackless regions of the world
their mystic banners are unfurled.

V

This Present Age

Poet's Quest

Who is the keeper of the flame?
Whoever the Muse has called by name
to cast words into a churning sea
until their sense and sound agree,
draw language thus infused with charm
out of the cauldron to disarm,
light up the castle, gather to bear
tidings of poetry sweet and clear.

The Planet

On weary earth with furrowed brow
whose patchwork coat of green and brown
in light of day seems woebegone
— it is by ancient sorrow worn —
a trace of wonder nightly steals
through space and splendor starlight reels
for all to see and dwell upon.

Like myriad thoughts
stars still glow
flash reports
in starry code
to cheer the world through surmise
a distant glory in the skies
winks to make its presence known.

How many eons stars have shone
while earth proceeding with wrinkled steps
straggles along a dreary coast
that tides erode
lest mortals ponder with downcast eye
the slow erosion of hope, and die.

San Francisco Universe

The city is sprawled like a giant web
woven of finest gold
by some uncanny instinct for design
on a ghostly canvas agleam and adrift in the night;
It is a radiant galaxy unrolled on a silent sea
propelled by a force unfathomed to a place unimagined —
a mirror image upside down in space.

I gaze transfixed at the fine-wrought scene
descend into the heart of a mystery
passengers disembark
disappear into shimmering canvas,
familiar constellations, roadways
like tendrils of light
where a city was once suspended
from a glittering height.

Leaving Ireland

On the shore of a distant sea
is the strangest land I've seen
A moonscape distilled from mist
sequestered in green.

A fitting place for time
to retrace its steps, wind
mystic hills, stone-marked fields
traversed by an olden race,

Who made this land of dreams
cradled in the waves
an eerie haunt for Druid chant
unfathomed thought and wistful song.

From the shore of that distant sea
from its mist-enshrouded past
that refuses to be forgotten
the ancient spell is cast.

Snowstorm in the Sierras

Ice-borne cherubs ermine furred
paint the forest softly blurred
in silent, falling, white array
veil the sylvan face of day.

Tumbling over the tallest peak
shaken out of the wintry deep
their legions multiply, skid and slide
down the trees on the windward side.

Against the blizzard the traveler sees
they know how to make the ground freeze —
how to attach clumps of snow
to winterize mountain trees.

Cavorting on hills that once were green
they seize the moment; are clearly keen
to saturate with entities
the very air the traveler breathes,

then skate away as darkness falls
on meadows slick as marble halls.
Morning finds the traveler gone,
over the world a frozen calm —

Except near branches hunched with cold
where streams in crunch of winter roll.
Ice angels rest, their labor done
white eyes glinting scan the sun.

Winter Night

I see the frost but do not feel the cold
I hear the wind but cannot feel it blow
for I have build a shelter from the storm
and there I dwell secure and warm.

I can only sense the bitter cold
advancing though the night so dark and wild
while I escape its icy grasp
for I am safe inside.

Now the winter sky begins to sway
as if to sweep the world I know away
I see the snow has fallen all around
and in the winter night the world is gone.

Tolerance

Said tree to meadow: "Do you know why
you are low and I am high
and over the very place you lie
trace leafy patterns on the sky?"

Replied the meadow: "It is so
you are high and I am low
while you decorate the clouds
I am trampled by the crowds.

"This is why you see me cry
in early hours of the day
until the kindly sun appears
to wipe my dewy tears away."

Said tree to meadow: "Can you explain
why I tower over the plain
and everyone looks up to me
don't you think it's destiny?"

Replied the meadow: "I agree
you are you and I am me."

Renewal

A breeze impresses the sunlit plain
bearing a dream of dormant grain
daring the light; shy leafy green
tries shades of red and tangerine.

Over the mountain and the sea
wherever the weariest heart may be
with blessed coolness fulfill your vow
spirit of Autumn, refresh us now.

Under the changing firmament
where earth, becalmed, sighs her lament
waken the forest and proclaim
the spirit of autumn on the plain:

Something will make the world seem new
summon the harvest and hope imbue
Come be one with the quickening scene
in fields of autumn courage glean.

Skirmish

In May the following is seen:
birds reconnoiter over fields
where the last trace of winter yields
to ingathering of green.

Slackened now her gusty pace
all senses know the land is free
of a long reign of austerity
so desultory her embrace —

Her ceaseless troubling kept at bay
foiled by a cycle, a warming trend
that brings it to a timely end —
disarmed by the revelry of May.

Resistance

Night spawns a quiet, impassive army
of conspiratorial trees
scheming under a dark canopy
guarding their secrets in close array
not conceding their thoughts to the non-
committal sky
(why should they?)
Shunning the wind's embrace —
sensing the mood of the earth
protecting the land
against the incursion of light
and depredation of day.

Night and Day — A Drama

Night like a curtain rises
on a grassy stage and fair
Out from the wings of morning
a drama will take place there.

However the story may go
the players shall have a voice
(too early it is to know
to weep or to rejoice).

A tale will be told each hour
too solemn to repeat
while day unfolds like a flower
(its fruit may be bitter or sweet).

Who knows if high endeavor
is destined to be rewarded
or if their long-sought prizes
will ever be awarded

Or if the envious night
shall have the final say
gathering to itself
the harvest of the day

When the curtain of night descends;
Despite its intricate schemes
when the drama finally ends
will nothing be left but dreams?

A National Anthem

I hear a solemn anthem
from nations far and strange
from every life evolving
in struggle and in change.

The anthem is resounding
and rising in the air
its harmony ascending
in tones so pure and clear,

As when the nations gather
who in their quest for peace
resolve to end their discord
and pray for war to cease;

It is the culmination
of every song once sung
in all the hearts of longing
from which the song is wrung
and every hope advancing —

Or when great congregations
in awe-filled worship blending
songs of adoration
tell of life unending;

It is a heavenly chorus of every song begun
in every scheme for progress
in which a race is run
by every person chancing
to face the blazing sun.

Emboldenment

Brave to dare the swift-winged flight
forsake a soft, familiar nest
you strive to touch the cloud-borne height.

Emblazoned on horizon's crest
the victory clear, the gamble won
your trophy is the sky and sun.

To earth and heaven you belong
to my spirit send your song.

VI

A World Beyond

A Writer's Prayer

Creator of celestial fire
by whose Word planets were cast into orbit
light flung upon earth like flame:
Give me the word that ignites.

Designer of sense and sound,
author of languages:
Enchant the word of conviction
to challenge the times with truth.

Embolden the word prophetic
that carves the persuasive phrase
as on tablets of stone
on the printed page.

Nativity I — Incarnation

As night gives birth to a billion stars
when day is gone
darkness is ever destined to be
the herald of dawn;
out of a place where hope is not
must hope be born.

So may the eye that is dim with tears
or doubt or pain
or some dark grief, rejoice to see
the Lord again;
Into a world where God is not
must God be born.

Nativity II —
Child of Highest Heaven

Behold a child is softly crying
who will save a world lost and dying,
the wooden trough where he is lain
precursor to a cross of pain.

The sorrow of God will soon be known
wholly to him when he is grown
that many might come to the throne of grace
men and women of every race,

Spirit-led and reconciled
by the daring mission of this child
now to the eye of faith resplendent
Infant, Savior, Love Transcendent.

The Magi Quest

To the Blessed One magi found their way
they knelt before Jesus that fateful day
and life was not as it was before
God was theirs forevermore.

Pray for those who journey today
though where and why they cannot say
their only wisdom — seeking to know
their only religion — daring to go.

Pray for them now: a dream can betray
pilgrim steps be led astray
pray for them now wherever they are
in city or desert who follow a star.

Tears

The rain, like torrents of tears
that fall in endless sorrow on the ground
to beat on recalcitrant stone in vain
or soak into the contrite earth
as if to wash the wayward planet clean,
reminds us of the tears that Jesus shed
over the wayward cities of the world
in sorrowful love outpoured.

John The Baptist

In the stillness of desert night
a man bore witness to the light
that by the lonely path he trod
all might know the ways of God.

John is a voice from long ago
who yet may speak to the world we know
where into the city we go and strive
to make the Kingdom of God arrive
by careful planning that God will bless
more than by prayer in the wilderness.

Under the sky of the urban night
though cities may blaze with man-made light
we long for the light that must have shone
for John in the desert all alone.

Mary Waiting on Easter Morning

Like Mary waiting on Easter morning
regretting a dream she thought was dead
in a world whence God had seemingly fled
leaving her weeping, perplexed, forlorn,
but daring to ask "Where is the Lord?"
and hearing at last the holy word,

We stand and wait by the empty tomb
knowing our hearts are dark and cold
sealed by the stone of doubt and gloom
refusing like Mary to be consoled.
Then we discover the One we seek
standing beside us and hear him speak.

An Easter Affirmation

The love that taught and healed in Galilee
in gracious word and deed is active still
has never ceased to be and never will.

The grief that bore our sins on Calvary
in anguish for the world is steadfast still
has never ceased to care and never will.

The power that won the Easter victory
in solemn joy and hope is moving still
over the human spirit and always will!

Retreat

This is why I keep a time apart
petition to reset my course by grace
by the spirit that indwells this holy place
I shall be stronger far when I depart.

For this is where I come with a heart of care
disheartened and irresolute until
into a sea where the tide of life runs full
I quiet my soul and cast the net of prayer.

Vision Quest

Unseen friend
whose spirit hovers over the human soul
as it once brooded over the sea
and called into being light and life
when the world was dark and dead,
Illumine our darkness with a word
in the pathless way we tread
who look to a light that none can see,
a face that is always hid.

Contemplation

Alone in the silence, I am blessed
Grant, oh God, my soul find rest
and prayer fulfill its ancient quest:

to flee dominion of earthly thought
stand where angels are Spirit-taught
for there most wondrous deeds are wrought —

such deeds as shape reality
that lame may leap and blind may see
nor leave the captive less than free:

to hear the most exalted word
that once the stars inchoate heard
and formed a blue celestial world —

resounded once in village streets
in human hearts, and still entreats
in wave on wave of history.

alone in the silence I would stay
to seek my God and find my way.

Ever Closer to The Source

I look to Thee within whose life
true life I see
ever closer to the source
of all I am and hope to be,

I look to Thee within whose light
true light I see
ever closer to the source
of all I know with certainty.

I look to Thee within whose love
true love I see
ever closer to the source
of all that means the most to me.

I look to Thee beyond whose world
a world I see
ever closer to the source
of all that is and is to be.

Into Silence

I dare my soul to mark the solemn hour
for healing of the world's disquietude
glean harvests of eternity
in fading tapestries of time
engage that higher realm where love abounds.

I dare my soul to free the wordless prayer
outpace swift odyssey of mind
unto thoughts aglow on the border of infinity
in silent steadfast journey
into the boundless glory of its home.

Holy Spirit Interceding

Romans 8:26, 27

Flame of far celestial fire
source of every high desire
promised gift of Christ's ascending
still a heavenly flame descending
on each soul with Spirit gifting,
We behold the shadows lifting,
flame that burns through old divisions —
race and gender — blessed visions
standing by us, ever pleading
by the Spirit interceding
Scrolls are opened that were sealed;
by their hidden words revealed
out from dungeons error wrought
liberating truth is brought;
out from prisons of despair
hope emerges free and fair
In word we cannot think or say
articulated when we pray;
in vistas promising and gleaming

the beautiful and true redeeming;
in anthems mute and long-forgotten
by the Spirit once begotten —
Music from a mystic shore
that we exult to hear once more —
We shall know the One who bore us
faithful intercessor for us
and oh, through dim and dreary skies
see the vision crystallize!

A Prayer for Women and Girls

Mother of all, who bore
Israel from the womb
whose ancient footsteps wore
a path to the empty tomb;
You are Wisdom and Word
whom once the world adored
for mother love and compassion.
Though we call you "Father" and "Lord"
still in the Book we find you
who mother-love does impart
that which is written in scripture
is graven in every heart.
You are the Holy Spirit
shelter us under your wings
deliver our souls from sorrow
and all that evil brings.
Mother of all, ever the same
gather us in
call us by name.

Look upon your daughters
we come to you in prayer
with sighs too deep to utter,
O Mother beyond compare
speak words of cheer to quicken
those of us who pray
with mind and spirit stricken
wipe our tears away.
Look upon your children
we know your word is true
send us forth to dream,
to envision the world anew.

A Prayer for the World

Maker of all; Giver of life;
Most Holy One;
live in each soul that Divine life
to which we are born.
By that divine flame
that first dispelled night
banish long ages
of fear and doubt
by that divine flame
that once flared most bright
enkindle our hearts
    To cast prophetic fire, like Christ
    by His might and redemptive love
    to lighten the terrible shadows cast
    by cruel strictures of the past,
    By faith to make the mountains move
    and bring the dawn of hope at last.
Maker of all: Giver of life;
Most Holy One;
live in each soul that divine life
to which we are born;

by that divine breath
that scattered the mist
brought form out of chaos
caught planets in space
By that divine breath
all of your children
renew in your likeness:
    To help create the world anew
    'til out of the mist of change shall rise
    nations who know and do your will
    who first conceived a paradise;
    By resolute prayer to dare to call
    a world into being, bright for all.

Defend Our Dream

If we have seen what we are meant to see
defend our vision; grant that it may rise
in other times and places known to Thee
to dawn like light of day on other eyes.

If we have seen the world that is to be
when we can do no more
defend the dream we dream because of Thee
and bring it safe to shore.

Altar Call

Line up and follow Jesus
our trust will be repaid
line up and follow Jesus
in a victory parade.

Some of us are in tatters
and some of us are in tears
some of us are stumbling
under a burden of years

Some are wounded by brambles
in thickets of regret
some of us can't *remember*
and some of us can't *forget.*

Line up and follow Jesus
the promise will be kept
that hope shall rise under the skies
where once we staggered and wept.

Soul Anchor

"We have this hope, a sure and steadfast anchor of the soul … "
— Hebrews 6:19 NRSV

Dust of stars is in my frame
God's love calls my name;
It calls me through life's finite span
to see the shape of an infinite plan.

I won't go down in a tide of chance
or drift on a sea of circumstance
for I know the One holding sway
over the night and coming day,

who bids me turn another page
who bids me take another stand,
Timeless over this present age
Sovereign over the promised land.

When a New Day Comes to Be

The sun rolls into a crimson ball
and tumbles into the sea.

The sun will escape its watery grave
when the next day comes to be.

Soul wraps itself in shadows now
the temporal light to flee

to be transformed when a new day dawns
and know that it is free.

VII

In Memoriam

Elaine: In Memoriam

Here in the yard in the summer breeze
plums and apricots line the trees,
fruit she would gather to give to me.
I remember the times that were.

How could I ever forget her?
How could I ever not recall
her cheerful welcome at the door
the family warmth her home assured.

A story, a joke, a word of praise
even when anguish seized her days
even when hours one by one
bore her closer to the unknown.

With stealthy tread upon the stairs
time marks the limit of our years
enters our familiar rooms
in our midst eternity looms.

Here in the yard in the summer breeze
I remember. A sister grieves.

Ascent

Dedicated to Neil Miranda, 1959-1982.

Shimmering in the stream of time
kindling every hope of mine
a light most welcome to my gaze
gleams afar
in some other world ablaze
in the heart of sun and star.

Though I fear to break the bond
known to limit and surround
I attain to higher ground
whereon the light is shining down;
I look around and all I see
a holy light is shining on.

It shines upon the vale of tears
lifts the burden of the years
sorrow-laden with the strife
that cast me down and took my life;
As in a long-forgotten dream
or in my highest memory
light and shadow — both sublime —
dance upon the waves of time.

VIII

Potpourri

Colored Balloons

Look! The balloons are everywhere!
They fill the sky!
They jostle each other in the air
and passersby!

They glance off folk who eye each other
then wink and pretend to run for cover
from jolly balloons that bounce and hover.

They prance and billow like round buffoons
on children who frolic in festive moons
of purple and green and mauve balloons.

The sky is filled with wonder today
I think the colored balloons should stay.

Under the Sea

Do you know what the sea wind brings?
Tidings of tiny folk with wings
    who make their home
    in a sapphire grove
    on the floor of the sea
    by a treasure trove.

Do you know what the waves confide
out of the luminescent brine?
They tell where tiny folk abide
who dance in an elfin chorus line
    and make their home
    in a sapphire grove
    on the floor of the sea
    by a treasure trove.

Do you know why the great sea shimmers?
It shimmers because of golden swimmers:
elfin, eldritch, eerie beings
who undulate with jeweled wings
dance all night with wild delight
circle the sea with diamond light
    and make their home
    in a sapphire grove
    on the floor of the sea
    by a treasure trove.

Do you know why the great sea sways
down a path of glittery waves?
The sea traverses opal shelves
stocked with gems by countless elves;
underwater queens and kings
undulate with jeweled wings
gather pearls to carpet their hall
shop in a ruby and garnet mall
    and make their home
    in a sapphire grove
    on the floor of the sea
    by a treasure trove.

Haiku

Rain slithers down rock
sand castles abandon beach
slide into the sea.

Gray amoeba clouds
red nuclei, spewed from flame
singe complacent sky.

Tufted hills stone rimmed
cling to precarious light
night a brushstroke away.

Heat Wave

A Pantoum

Though wavelets tumble over coast
Shore cannot slake its thirst
Sand bakes in furnace of the sun
Nature exacts its toll.

Shore cannot slake its thirst
Heat is unrelenting in its hold
Nature exacts its toll
Vacationers seek shelter in the shade.

Heat is unrelenting in its hold
Wilting in the sultry atmosphere
Vacationers seek shelter in the shade
Scorched by season's piercing ray.

Wilting in the sultry atmosphere
Grass melts into yellow haze
Scorched by season's piercing ray
Earth cannot find relief.

Grass melts into yellow haze
Sand bakes in furnace of the sun
Earth cannot find relief
Though wavelets tumble over coast.

Come Spin the Arrow

This is where the truth lies
it lies beneath the ground
shovel to earth, mind to mind
this is where truth is found.

This is where ashes mark a place
where people huddled around;
a crackling fire against the cold
was all the truth they found.

We sense their fear and feel their plight,
their yearning for the ambient light
we tremble and stand along with them
and spin the arrow of time again.

This is where the truth lies
hidden in the ground
ink on parchment, mind on mind
this is where truth is found.

Words imprinted on leather scrolls
spirit to spirit, we pray for the souls
of all those learned and pious men
and spin the arrow of time again.

This is where the truth is found:
in songs of ancient bards;
how strange to hear them singing
after all these years.

Where the Arrow Came to Rest

Here I wait with bated breath
to see where the arrow will come to rest.
It veers to the left, then to the right,
coaxes the future from where it lies coiled,
ready to spring, and not to be foiled.